PIANO • VOCAL • GUITAR

CHART HITS

of 2012-2013

ISBN 978-1-4803-3796-1

HAL•LEONARD
CORPORATION
7777 W. BLUEMOUND RD. P.O. BOX 13819 MILWAUKEE, WI 53213

WITHDRAWN

Visit Hal Leonard Online at
www.halleonard.com

THE A TEAM

Words and Music by
ED SHEERAN

4

AS LONG AS YOU LOVE ME

Words and Music by JUSTIN BIEBER,
SEAN ANDERSON, NASRI ATWEH,
RODNEY JERKINS and ANDRE LINDAL

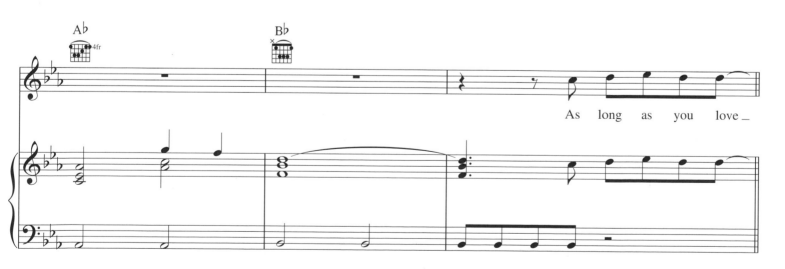

Additional Lyrics

Rap: I don't know if this makes sense but you're my hallelujah.
Give me a time and place, I'll rendezvous it. I'll fly you to it.
I'll beat you there. Girl, you know I got you, us, trust.
A couple things I can't spell without you.
Now we on top of the world, 'cause that's just how we do.
Used to tell me sky's the limit, now the sky's our point of view.
Man, we steppin' out like, whoa, oh God, cameras point and shoot.
Ask me what's my best side, I stand back and point at you.
You, you the one that I argue with, feel like I need a new girl to be bothered with.
But the grass ain't always greener on the other side, it's green where you water it.
So I know we got issues, baby, true, true, true, but I'd rather work on this wit' you
Than to go ahead and start with someone new. As long as you love me.

BLOW ME
(One Last Kiss)

Words and Music by ALECIA MOORE
and GREG KURSTIN

Driving Dance beat

50 WAYS TO SAY GOODBYE

Words and Music by PAT MONAHAN,
ESPEN LIND and AMUND BJORKLUND

*Recorded a half step lower.

I wan-na live a thou-sand lives ___ with you. ___ I wan-

HO HEY

Words and Music by JEREMY FRAITES
and WESLEY SCHULTZ

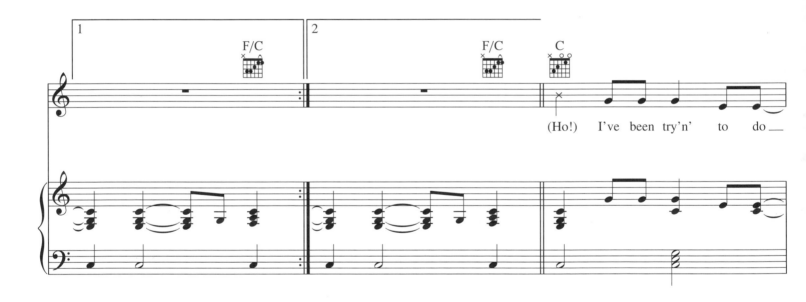

LITTLE TALKS

Words and Music by NANNA HILMARSDOTTIR
and RAGNAR THORHALLSSON

*Recorded a half step higher.

Both: You're

gone,   gone,   gone   a - way;___   I   watched   you   dis - ap - pear.___
torn,   torn,   torn   a - part;___   there's   noth - ing   we   can   do.___

44

I KNEW YOU WERE TROUBLE.

Words and Music by TAYLOR SWIFT,
SHELLBACK and MAX MARTIN

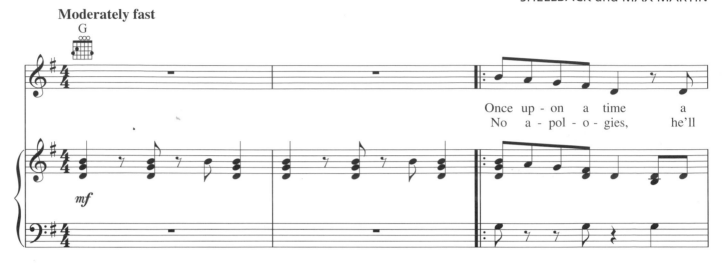

I WON'T GIVE UP

Words and Music by JASON MRAZ
and MICHAEL NATTER

*Guitarists: Tune 6th string down to D.

IT'S TIME

Words and Music by DANIEL REYNOLDS,
BENJAMIN McKEE and DANIEL SERMON

LIVE WHILE WE'RE YOUNG

Words and Music by RAMI YACOUB,
SAVAN KOTECHA and CARL FALK

ONE MORE NIGHT

Words and Music by ADAM LEVINE,
JOHAN SCHUSTER and MAX MARTIN

Moderate Reggae groove

Ooh _____ ooh ooh ooh ooh ooh ooh.

Ooh _____ ooh ooh ooh ooh ooh ooh. You and I go

hard at each oth - er like we're go - ing to war. _____ You and I go

"no," but my bod - y keeps on tell - ing you, "yes." _____ Try to tell you,

LOCKED OUT OF HEAVEN

Words and Music by BRUNO MARS,
ARI LEVINE and PHILIP LAWRENCE

With energy

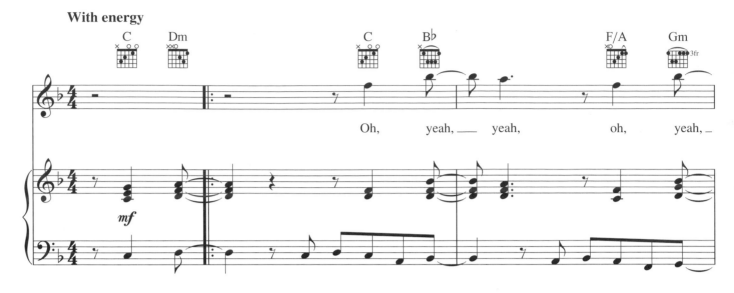

D.S. al Coda

SKYFALL

from the Motion Picture SKYFALL

Words and Music by ADELE ADKINS
and PAUL EPWORTH

SOME NIGHTS

Words and Music by JEFF BHASKER,
ANDREW DOST, JACK ANTONOFF
and NATE RUESS

Moderately, with a March feel

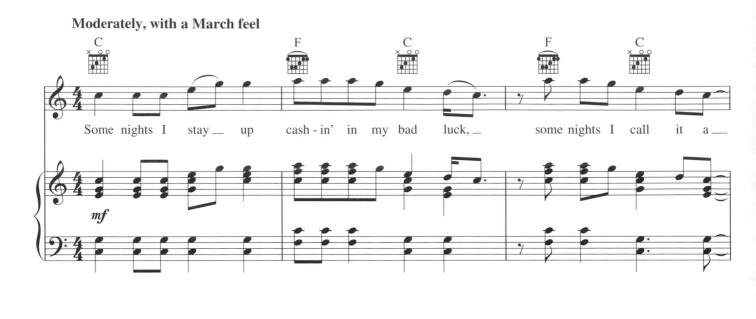

Some nights I stay __ up cash-in' in my bad luck, __ some nights I call it a __

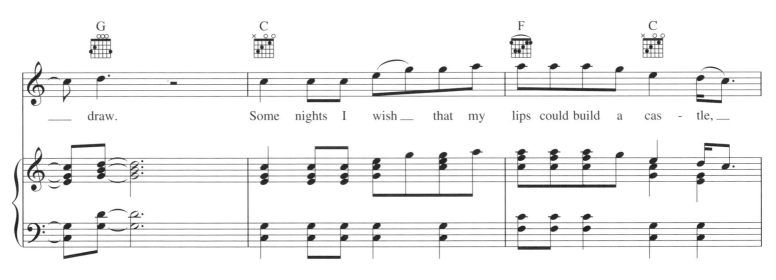

__ draw. Some nights I wish __ that my lips could build a cas - tle, __

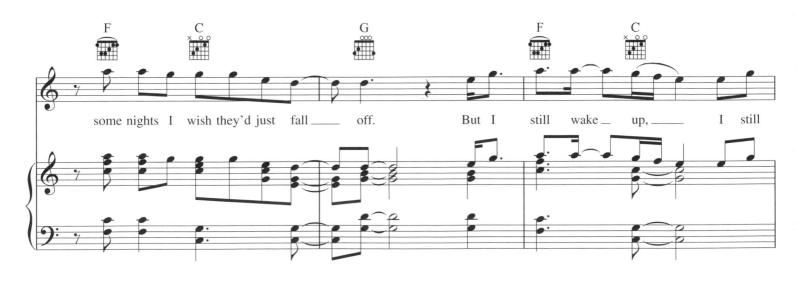

some nights I wish they'd just fall __ off. But I still wake __ up, __ I still

To Coda ⊕

This is it ___ boys, this is war. What ___ are we wait - in' for? ___ Why ___ don't we break the rules al -

rea - dy? ___ I was nev - er one ___ to be - lieve the hype, ___

save that ___ for the black and white. I try twice as hard ___ and I'm half as liked but

105

TOO CLOSE

Words and Music by ALEX CLAIRE
and JIM DUGUID

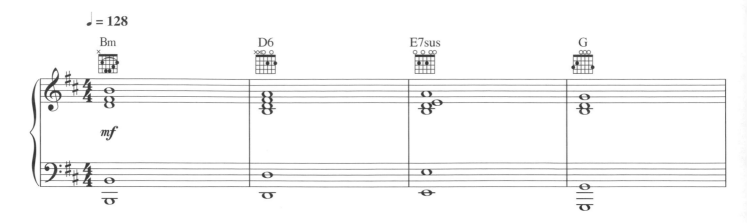

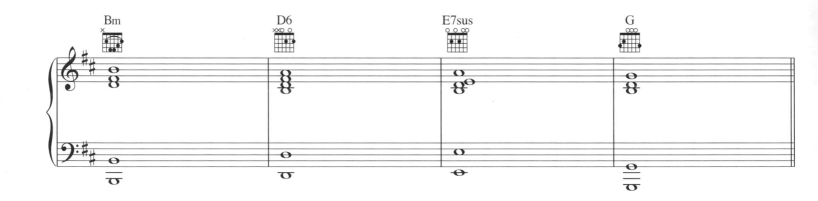

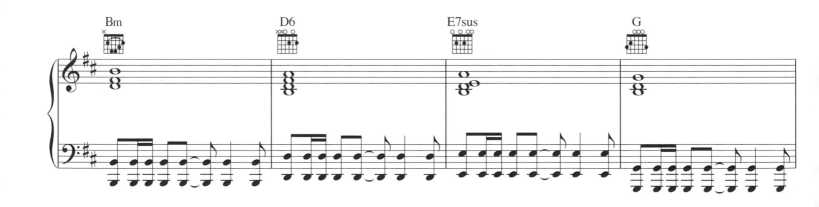

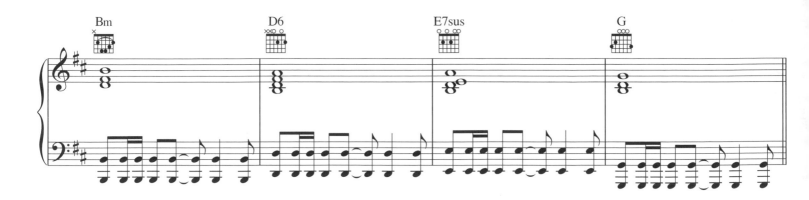

WE ARE NEVER EVER GETTING BACK TOGETHER

Words and Music by TAYLOR SWIFT,
SHELLBACK and MAX MARTIN

I re-mem-ber when we broke _ up, the first time, say-in' this is it, I've had e-nough. But 'cause like we

had-n't seen each oth-er in a month when you said you need-ed space. What?

118

THE ULTIMATE SONGBOOKS

HAL•LEONARD

PIANO PLAY-ALONG

These great songbook/CD packs come with our standard arrangements for piano and voice with guitar chord frames plus a CD.

The CD includes a full performance of each song, as well as a second track without the piano part so you can play "lead" with the band! Volumes 86 and beyond also include the Amazing Slow Downer technology so PC and Mac users can adjust the recording to any tempo without changing the pitch!

HAL•LEONARD®
CORPORATION
7777 W. BLUEMOUND RD. P.O. BOX 13819
MILWAUKEE, WISCONSIN 53213

Visit Hal Leonard Online at
www.halleonard.com

Prices, contents and availability subject to change without notice.
Disney characters and artwork © Disney Enterprises, Inc.

0512